SOCKET BAYONETS

A History and Collector's Guide

Graham Priest

AMBERLEY

First published 2016

Amberley Publishing
The Hill, Stroud
Gloucestershire, GL5 4EP

www.amberley-books.com

Copyright © Graham Priest, 2016

The right of Graham Priest to be identified as
the Author of this work has been asserted in
accordance with the Copyrights, Designs and
Patents Act 1988.

ISBN 978 1 4456 4991 7 (print)
ISBN 978 1 4456 4992 4 (ebook)

British Library Cataloguing in Publication Data.
A catalogue record for this book is available from
the British Library.

Typesetting by Amberley Publishing.
Printed in the UK.

Contents

Acknowledgements

Particular thanks to 'Tony' Foster and John Humphries for ongoing help and support. Appreciation to (late) Michael Bird, Cyril Cabanas, Brian Cavill, Derek Complin, Krzysztof Cieciura, Roger Evans, Shawn Gibson, Erik Goldstein, Jeff Hayes, Per Holmback, Jean-Louis Legens, (late) 'Dick' Marsden, Hector J. Meruelo, Christian Méry, Ron Reeves, Pierre Renoux, Juan Luis Calvó Pascual and Robert Wilkinson-Latham for the many illustrations. Gratitude to staff for aid and access to the following organisations:– Armémuseum, Stockholm; Banco Bilbao Vizcaya Argentaria, Madrid; Collection of Richard P. W. Williams, USA; Dean and Authorities of Westminster Abbey, London (D. Tony Trowles); Earl of Dalkeith Collection, Boughton House, Northants (Hon. R. W. J. M. D. Scott, Earl of Dalkeith and Gareth Fitzpatrick); Musée d'archéologie et d'histoire locale, Denain, France; Palace Armoury, Grand Master's Palace, Malta (Robert Cassar and (Late) Mike Stroud); Pitt Rivers Museum, Oxford (Marina de Alarcón); Riflecraft Ltd (Andrew Evans-Hendrick); RMAS Archives (C. Gray); Surrey Infantry Museum, Clandon Park, Surrey; Trustees of the Weapons Collection, Land Warfare Centre, Warminster, Wiltshire and World Wide Arms Ltd (Les and Merita Rawlins). Thanks to *Bayonet Notebook* individuals who also contributed.

Captions provide details. Unattributed items are in the author's collection. Every attempt has been made to seek permission for copyright material. However, if copyright material has inadvertently been used without permission or acknowledgement, apologies are proffered and the necessary corrections will be made at the first opportunity.

To Freddie, Jessica, Sonny, Vincent and Zara. Grandpa's little helpers!

Introduction

As you have chosen this book there is a high probability that you can identify a 'bayonet', but what is a 'socket' bayonet? The *Oxford English Dictionary* defines 'bayonet' as, 'a sword-like stabbing blade which may be fixed to the muzzle of a rifle for use in hand-to-hand fighting.'

One electric lightbulb attachment has a 'bayonet fitting'. This gives the answer. The hollow cylindrical holder has twin 'zig-zag' slots for two lugs on the bulb. Insertion and twist (with internal spring) secures the item. A bayonet tube fits over the smaller barrel of the firearm. The (usually single) stud, sometimes a foresight, slots into the 'socket'. The blade is offset from the barrel to allow passage for a bullet. Originally this displacement allowed the user to muzzle-load his musket without blade damage to his hand.

Not always 'sword-like', the socket bayonet converted a longarm into a rickety spear. With a single-shot firelock an emergency blade was useful in time of need. Tactics and applications developed as the arm evolved. National characteristics and multi-purpose functions appeared. Performance in conflict developed a momentum of its own. The initial defensive role also became offensive. Very rarely did bayonet-armed adversaries trade blows despite training method assumptions that they might. Often the threat of the weapon, rather than its deployment, won the day. Physical handling strengthened muscles and inculcated an aggressive attitude. From the late seventeenth century until today, socket bayonets were more often used in single combat situations.

Above: **Fig. 1** Sword-bayonet, Pattern 1907, Mark I.

Right: **Fig. 2** Bayonet socket with mortise.

Fig. 3 French 1703-style *bayonette à douille* on musket barrel. (Courtesy of Palace Armoury, Malta)

Fig. 4 Flintlock carbine and bayonet from Shirburn Castle by H. Delany *c.* 1713. (Courtesy of World Wide Arms Ltd)

Fig. 5 English 'plug bayonet' *c.* 1683. Reused blade dated 1647. (Courtesy of Pitt Rivers Museum, Oxford)

Fig. 6 English 'India Pattern' bayonet, Brown Bess style.

Fig. 7 British bayonet training at the Land Warfare Centre, Warminster 2011.

More sophisticated blade to barrel attachment methods developed as technology improved. The elephant in the room was the need for bullets to pass through sockets. Even when multi-shot, breech-loaded firearms appeared the bayonet survived. From eighteenth-century battlefield panoramas (where artists drew bayonets as cranked lines), through faded carte-de-viste of anxious American Civil War combatants with prominent rifle-muskets, to current television footage of troops in Iraq or Afghanistan, the socket bayonet is found. As a last vestige of personal-level early bladed warfare, the bayonet has survived and flourished for over 300 years. This is the story of the 'socket bayonet'.

Fig. 8 French locking ring of 1777.

Left: **Fig. 9** Recruitment images of grenadier and private 2nd Foot (Queen's Royal Regiment) *c.* 1715. (Courtesy of Surrey Infantry Museum, Clandon Park)

Below: **Fig. 10** 'Bayonet, L3A1' with 'Scabbard, L1A1', used on 'Rifle, L85A1' in Iraq.

The Origin of the Bayonet

Where a first musketeer inserted a knife into a muzzle to create a pike will never be known. Probably in the sixteenth century, the originator a hunter, and the Basque region of the Pyrenean Mountains the location. Dangerous game, for example wild boar, needed to be deterred if a single round had failed to kill. Men soon realised the military potential of the combination arm. At that time, the heavy matchlock *arquebus*, with a forked rest to give support, was often flanked by pikemen to provide protection during the slow recharging procedure. Arrival of the lighter, more portable *fusil*, with its flintlock mechanism, allowed a specialist knife to be deployed. England adopted the system on 14 March 1662. The appendage became a *baggonet* or *bayonet*. The etymology of the word would fill a book in itself. Readers interested in how the name developed are directed to Captain Sir David Sibbald Scott's lecture 'On the history of the bayonet' from the Royal United Services Institution, 27 May 1863. In the 1570s the French word *bayonnette* described a utility knife, probably from the cutlers of Bayonne adjacent to the Basque region. A published reference of 1647 linked the blades to military firearms. Titles derived from geographical locations can be compared with other commodities, e.g. *Cheddar* – an English village cheese. Modern historians used the term 'plug bayonet'.

Fig. 11 King Charles III of Spain with fusil and plug bayonet by Francisco de Goya (1786–1788). (Banco Bilbao Vizcaya Argentaria Collection, Madrid, Spain)

Fig. 12 Musketeer with matchlock *arquebus*. (Originally printed in *The exercise of armes for caliures, muskettes, and pikes*, 1608)

Fig. 13 First drawing of *bayonnette*. (Originally printed in *Traites des Armes*, 1678)

Fig. 14 Decorative late Spanish hunting plug bayonet *c.* 1800. (Courtesy of Pitt Rivers Museum, Oxford)

Originally, soldiers carried bayonets and swords together as sidearms. Technologists were unable to produce standardised barrel diameters so tapered hilts fitted all muzzles. Muskets were discharged in volleys and bayonets inserted to repel or attack an enemy if there was insufficient time to reload. English drill books for this procedure arrived in 1675. By the 1685 Battle of Sedgemoor, pikes were less used and by 1705 were obsolete. If 'plugged', the musket could not be reloaded or discharged. This disadvantage was seen in 1689, at the Battle of Killiecrankie, when the Highlanders' charge was too fast for royal troops to fix bayonets. Heavy defeat followed.

'Ring' or 'socket' bayonets evolved to solve the difficulty. France created a workable design by 1669. A 1697 engraving showed a long 'spear' cranked from a slotted tubular socket. This device allowed unimpeded use of the firearm and a defensive blade at all times. Battlefield tactics changed.

Fig. 15 Full stocked 'doglock' musket from the reign of William and Mary (1689–1702), as used at Killiecrankie. This had a plug bayonet (Courtesy of the Trustees of the Weapons Collection, Land Warfare Centre, Warminster)

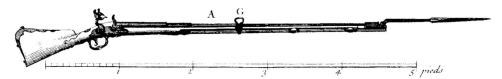

Fig. 16 1697 flintlock musket with 'spear' socket bayonet. (Originally printed in P. Saint Remy's *Memoires d' Artillerie, Vol. 1*, 1697)

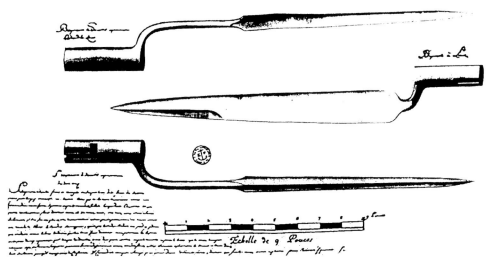

Fig. 17 Alternative *bayonette à douille* designs for French Marines, from a 1703 French drawing. (Courtesy of the Archives Nationale, Paris)

Fig. 18 Swiss spear bayonet *c.* 1720.

Fig. 19 Flat bladed socket bayonet of the French 1703 type. (Courtesy of Pierre Renoux)

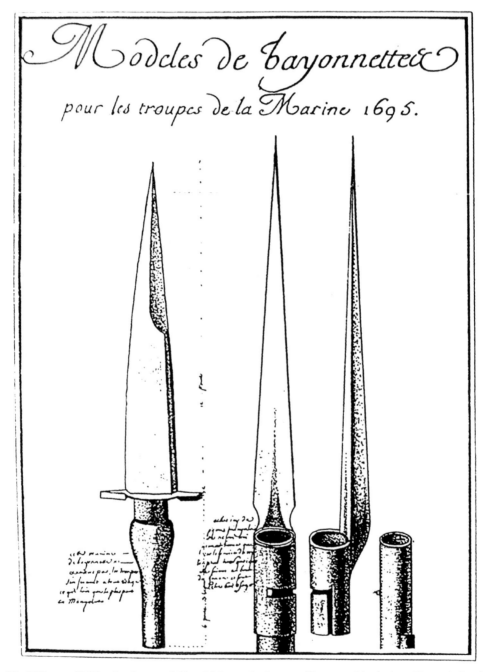

Fig. 20 Proposed 1695 socket design with French Marine plug bayonet. (Courtesy of the Archives Nationale, Paris)

Plug to Socket Bayonet

Military plug bayonets of wood, brass and steel, or more precious materials, evolved over seven decades. Cutlers provided a variety of blade forms and lengths, some reused from swords or daggers. Most had cross-guards and tapered hilts. Guards might have utilitarian quillons for hand protection and leverage on the musket, some designed as screwdrivers or 'hammers' for knapping flints. Grips of timber, bone or ivory provided purchase without damage to the bore. Smaller than barrel-diameter metal pommels capped the handles. Late seventeenth-century 'standard' military forms developed together with decorative commercial designs for officers or hunters. Many outlived the firearms as sidearms. Elegant appearance, precious metals, profuse blade markings and inscriptions made survivors desirable to collectors.

Rarer, and so harder to collect, were transitional types, described by Grose as '... of the dagger kind which handles then had two rings, fixed to them for the admission of the barrel of the piece.'

The idea of a 'ring' bayonet evolved from this reference to Queen Anne's (1665–1714) dragoon escort. Was 'ring' an alternative word for 'socket' and part of the bayonet or firearm?

One French matchlock musket had twin stock-bands with a stiletto-type bayonet 'plugged' outside the barrel. Bayonets with muzzle-rings on their guards and hilt spring catches appeared.

Very rare was the 'socket-dagger'. Unlike previous designs, the hilt was never intended for muzzle insertion. A concave pommel and grip fitted beside a firearm's barrel. Attached to the guard was a socket slotted for sight or lug. Wooden-gripped musket versions matched walnut- or ivory-hilted carbine designs. Robert Killigrew's carved marble funeral monument in Westminster Abbey, London by Francis Bird *c.* 1710 provided a context. Here bayonets were attached to flintlock carbines. Killigrew had his own squadron of dragoons until killed at the Battle of Almanza, 25 April 1707. The 1706 *Schedule of Clothing* for Killigrew's dragoons mentioned, '... split-socket bayonets to serve over a full-bored musket.'

Fig. 21 Early French plug bayonet without quillons and deep fuller, *c.* 1670. (Courtesy of Pitt Rivers Museum, Oxford)

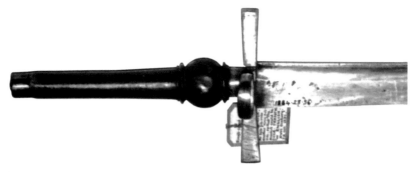

Fig. 22 Swiss/German hybrid plug 'ring' bayonet for outside musket barrel *c.* 1690. Quillons act as hammer and screwdriver. (Courtesy of Pitt Rivers Museum, Oxford)

Fig. 23 Spring catch on hilt. (Courtesy of Pitt Rivers Museum, Oxford)

Fig. 24 Ivory-hilted 'socket-dagger' for officer's fusil or hunting carbine *c.* 1700.

Fig. 25 Concave grip and socket of above intended for outside the barrel.

Fig. 26 Steel muzzle-ring and integral socket of wooden-gripped 'socket-dagger' *c.* 1700. (Earl of Dalkeith Collection, Boughton House, Northants)

Fig. 27 Engraving of Brigadier General Robert Killigrew's monument in Westminster Abbey. Dated 1707, it was carved a few years later. (Originally printed in *Westmonasterium or the History of the Abbey Church of St Peter's Westminster*, 1742)

Fig. 28 Top left-hand corner, with 'socket-dagger', of the marble monument by Francis Bird *c.* 1710. (Courtesy of Dean and Authorities of Westminster Abbey)

Brass- and wooden-gripped musket dimensioned examples resembled the marble depictions, but may have fitted dragoon firelocks. William Justice, registered in the London Cutler's Company 1664, marked one.

Fig. 29 Socket, grooved hilt and pommel of a musket bore 'socket-dagger', similar to the previous image. (Courtesy of Derek Complin)

Fig. 30 The diminutive socket of the previous bayonet. (Courtesy of Derek Complin)

Fig. 31 London Cutler's 'Anchor' mark assigned to William Justice, 20 April 1664, on the bayonet seen on page 18. (Courtesy of Derek Complin)

Fig. 32 Walnut-gripped, all steel 'socket-dagger' for fusil or carbine (Earl of Dalkeith Collection, Boughton House, Northants)

A refined, steel, mounted bayonet, probably for an officer's fusil, was at Boughton House. General John, Second Duke of Montagu, Master General of Ordnance in 1740, possibly acquired it with many similar vintage weapons.

After 1679, London cutler John Garner created a most elaborate example with an ivory grip, brass socket, tiny 'winged figure' quillons and hollow, ovoid pommel. Slight constructional imperfections suggested this was a converted dagger. The small-bored socket was not intended for robust military issue but for a fusil or hunting weapon.

The concept of a knife or sword with a socket attached for use as a bayonet resurfaced in the nineteenth century. The principle was an evolutionary diversion. Late seventeenth-century technologists found that a cranked blade, offset from the socket, was more efficient. The 'socket bayonet' had arrived.

Fig. 33 Ivory-hilted 'socket-dagger' with brass socket inlet into blade.

Fig. 34 Double 'flaming sword' London Cutler's mark. Assigned to John Garner on 23 October 1679.

Fig. 35 'Winged-figure' brass quillon. The cherubic archer was possibly Eros. The style was popular around 1700.

Formative Years – 1690 to 1730

Although early socket bayonet design was established by the beginning of the eighteenth century, the technologies used varied considerably. The principal developers in Europe comprised of dukedoms, kingdoms, palatinates, principalities, states etc. Some were in larger power-blocks led by ruling elites. As designers tried to secure a bladed tube outside a musket barrel with free passage for a bullet, solutions varied. Larger, or technically advanced, kingdoms, e.g. Britain, France, the Holy Roman Empire, Spain, Russia and Sweden produced prototypes, some with limited survival. To collectors these remain elusive and thus very desirable. As accessories to particular firearms, the innovations were intended to produce a complete 'bayonet-piece'.

By 1692, Sweden, plentifully supplied with iron ore, timber (meaning charcoal and fuel) and water (power), had adopted a plug bayonet with an external spring and muzzle ring. (Fig. 23) From 1696 until 1731, a range of distinctive socket bayonets appeared. Short (53-mm) sockets projected flat double-edged blades (655 mm) from the muzzles. Offset, for hand access when the flintlock *Musköt m/1696s* were loaded, these blades were parallel-sided from muzzles to tapered symmetrical points. Attachment was by a three-step mortise and wing-bolt. Models 1699, 1701, 1704, 1716, 1717, 1725, 1727 and 1731, from Jönköping, Norköping, Örebro, Ronneby, Stockholm and Wira, varied. Some blades fitted to the left of the barrel.

In 1669 Sébastien Vauban proposed French socket bayonets, but a shankless 1695 Marine type (Fig. 20) was displaced by a 'spear' or '*lame tranchantes*' (knife blade) in 1703. The latter was criticised for being unwieldy, weaker, dangerous to the hand and liable for misuse as a tool. An engraved decorative 'shield' or 'apron' at the shank base

Fig. 36 Swedish *hylsbajonett* for *Musköt m/1696* with squared shank and wing-bolt (Courtesy of Armémuseum, Stockholm)

become a Gallic feature. From 1691 to 1730s spear versions, often from the arsenal at Tulle, served with the Compagnies franches in Nouvelle France (Canada). By 1717, the *fusils de soldat* had shorter triangular-bladed designs. These retained uncollared sockets, two-step mortises and shortened shanks. Unfullered blades were 14 pouces (365 mm) long. These became the first official French issues as *baïonnettes modèles 1717*. By 1728 the lightened blades had concavities or fullers.

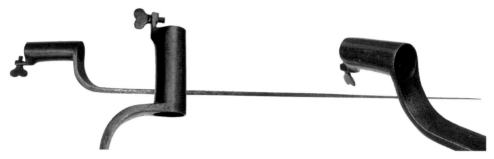

Fig. 37 Swedish *hylsbajonett* for *Musköt m/1716*, similar to *m/1704*. Note the blade formation and wing-bolt. (Courtesy of Jeff Hayes)

Fig. 38 French flat *lame tranchantes* (knife blade) bayonet used on *c.* 1703 army and galley muskets.

Fig. 39 Distinctive French engraved 'shield' or 'apron' on *baïonnette modèle 1746*. (Courtesy of Pierre Renoux)

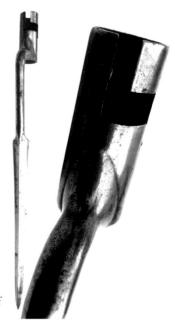

Fig. 40 'Spear' bayonet with 'shield', probably Swiss, similar to those of *Compagnies franches* in *Nouvelle France* (Canada).

Fig. 41 French *baïonnette modèle 1717* for *fusil de soldat*. Unfullered triangular-sectioned blade and typical 'L' slot. One has shield decoration. (Courtesy of Cyril Cabanas and Pierre Renoux)

Fig. 42 The concave fullers of French *baïonnette modèle 1728*.

Britain's association with the Low Countries during the Wars of the Grand Alliance (1689–97) and Spanish Succession (1702–14) cross-fertilised ideas, so many 'Dutch' weapons were similar. Before the Board of Ordnance's 1722 directive was enforced in the 1740s, regimental colonels were able to adopt any adequate bayonet as there was no prescribed model. These 'private purchase' types, charged to government funds, varied. The earliest issued with 'Snaphance Musquetts Ordanry' [sic] had unreinforced sockets, relatively weak, squared shanks and leaf-shaped, flattened lozenge-sectioned blades. Three-step slots fitted foresights on barrels. Numbered examples to particular weapons, and one owned by 'Phillip Papillon of Lubenham Esq', dated to 1700–20. Blade lengths began to approach 17 inches (434 mm). Shanks were sometimes welded to sockets to form functional but decorative shields.

Zig-zag slots, mated with sights to orientate blades on lock sides, were open-ended to allow adjustment for barrel diameter. As tubes distorted easily, collars provided rigidity. Studs then had to pass through 'bridges'. Heavy 'cannon-muzzle' forms were replaced by simple 'rings'. Weak shanks were also made longer and more rounded to give strength. 'Flatt' [sic] blades from Ordnance accounts became 'hollow' around 1715. Triangular-sectioned, possibly ex-sword blades, were fullered on outer faces. More support in unreinforced leather scabbards was provided by a distinct 'ledge' between blade and shank.

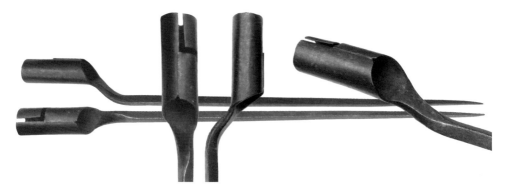

Fig. 43 Rare 'split-socket' (three-step slot) stiletto-bladed bayonet for bottom-stud musket. Possibly a colonel's purchase from Low Countries *c.* 1700. (Courtesy of Jeff Hayes)

Fig. 44 A 'flatt' bayonet for Queen Anne, 'Pattern 1703'-style musket from Papillon Hall. Bayonet socket and barrel marked 'Phillip Papillon of Lubenham Esq'. (Collection of Richard P. W. Williams, USA)

Fig. 45 A small-sized 'flatt' bayonet from a carbine by Henry Delany *c.* 1714, ex-Shirburn Castle, Oxfordshire. (Courtesy of World Wide Arms Ltd)

Fig. 46 'Colonel's purchase' flat bayonet with cannon barrel collar. (Courtesy of Krzysztof Cieciura)

Fig. 47 *c.* 1720 English 'colonel's purchase' bayonet, with unusual blade section and 'ledge' for scabbard support. Sword-blade-style deep groove on inner blade face. The shank welded to the socket. (Courtesy of John Humphries)

Holy Roman Empire models (now Austria, Germany and parts of Belgium) favoured 'split-socket' types. This modern term for open seamed tubes allowed adjustment to fit non-standard barrels. Precise details of their origin was uncertain, but archaeological proof that particular models were at the Battle of Denain on 14 July 1712 was dredged from the River Scheldt. One form, complete with 'langet', was cut and folded from a flat sheet of iron. The knife blades were typical of a style used by the Knights of the Order of St John in Malta. Simplified *Dillenbajonnet* from 1680–1700 were known from illustrations. Others were constructed from several components or with scabbard ledges. Smaller states, for example Brandenburg and Saxony, adopted French designs. Large 'machete' blades were also used.

Above: **Fig. 48** Simple, possibly Austrian, 'split-socket' made from folded iron. (Courtesy of Shawn Gibson)

Left: **Fig. 49** Two bayonets dredged from River Scheldt after Battle of Denain, 14 July 1712. On the left, a 'colonel's purchase' type bayonet, probably Dutch or British, with a distinctive slanted muzzle. On the right, a Germanic split-socket bayonet. The langet part of forging. (Courtesy of Musée d'archéologie et d'histoire locale, Denain)

Fig. 50 Split-socket bayonet, with open seam and langet, from the Knights of St John, Malta. Over 180 remain in Grand Master's Palace, Valletta.

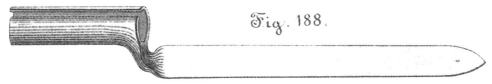

Fig. 51 Simplified split-socket *Dillenbajonnet* without langet used by German states. (Originally published in *Die Geschichtliche Entwickelung der Handfeuerwaffe*, 1886)

Fig. 52 Holy Roman Empire split-socket bayonet with langet riveted to blade. (Courtesy of Jeff Hayes)

Fig. 53 Split-socket bayonet with scabbard ledge on blade. (Courtesy of Shawn Gibson)

Fig. 54 Germanic (Saxony, *c.* 1715) bayonet with machete-style blade.

Fig. 55 Spanish *bayoneta de cubo, 1,700* for *Fusil Para Infanteria, 1,700.* This had an internal leaf spring to lock over stud on barrel. (Originally published in *Modelos Portatiles de Avancarga 1717/1843*, 1975)

Russia continued to use plug bayonets until the socket model of 1731. The earliest known Spanish design was for the *Fusil Para Infanteria, 1,700* in the Museo Militar del Castillo de Montjuich, Barcelona. The snaplocked musket had a very advanced bayonet with 556-mm blade attached directly to the 107-mm-long socket. This used a short three-step mortise and an internal leaf spring to align the blade beneath the muzzle of the firearm.

National Characteristics *c.* 1750

By the mid-eighteenth century, most European countries had adopted the flintlock musket and socket bayonet as their primary small arm. Larger nations created government facilities, for example France's 'Manufacture Royale d'Armes Blanches d'Alsace', Klingenthal (1731) with their own distinctive designs. Simultaneously commercial enterprises in Birmingham, Charleville, Herzberg, Liège, London, Madrid, Maubeuge, Milan, San Sebastián, St Étienne, Solingen, Suhl, Toledo, Tulle, Vienna etc. utilised metalwork skills and added bayonets to their product ranges. These centres were usually linked to adequate supplies of raw materials and water power. Guilds established working practices, but ordnance purchasers introduced checks and balances to ensure quality. Bayonet-makers specialised in the techniques of forging, welding, filing and polishing, so a single weapon passed through several hands before the 'viewer' accepted or rejected it. Marks were applied throughout the process to identify tradesmen for payment (or censure) and check the bayonet was of a required standard.

A finished blade would be provided with a scabbard from a different group of artisans and 'set up' on the firearm by another gun maker's organisation. As early as 28 November 1703, the Ministère de la Marine in France stated, '… all the sockets have to be of the same caliber and that the slot for the stud will need to be of the same length and width for all the bayonets to be fitted to any musket …'

However, the target of interchangeability waited another 100 years! Engraved alpha-numerics on both bayonet and firelock united the unique combination. Regimental markings demonstrated ownership.

These marks help the modern collector date and identify a bayonet, but so do particular idiosyncrasies of design associated with each country.

Most nations provided an open-ended socket, but the number of 'legs' in the mortise varied from two to four. Saxony often used the latter. The position of the stud/sight on

Fig. 56 Bottom: English 'Land Pattern'. Top: French *baïonnette du règlement de 1750*. Inset are different blade shoulders and an English collar.

Fig. 57 French blade grinders at work in water-powered manufactory *c.* 1751. (Originally published in Diderot and d'Alembert's *Encyclopédie, ou dictionnaire raisonné des sciences, des arts et des métiers*, 1751)

Fig. 58 Ricasso markings. Left to right: English 'Land Pattern', French *baïonnette modèle 1763* and Austrian *c.* 1740 model. 'P' may be Birmingham proof symbol (left). 'A. Nicholas' (centre) was maker or retailer. The 'crown' is the smith's marking (right).

Fig. 59 'Land Pattern' musket bayonet and scabbard numbered '50'. Made by James Freeman, London *c.* 1735. Ex-Shirburn Castle, Oxfordshire. (Courtesy of World Wide Arms Ltd.)

Fig. 60 'No. 1643' engraved on *c.* 1750 Saxon bayonet.

Fig. 61 Different mortise arrangements for top and bottom studs. Left to right: Malta *c.* 1730 'L' top; Austria *c.* 1740 'L' extended sub; France *c.* 1750 three-step sub; Norway *c.* 1730 three-step top (holes for handle), and Saxony *c.* 1750 four-step top.

the barrel also decided the position of the slot. Many Continental countries favoured sub-barrel tenons, but England and the Low Countries mainly used foresights. Russia adopted a side lug. Countries usually orientated bayonet blades to the lock sides of muskets so a smoother surface was against the user. Ramrods below muzzles deterred blades from this location, although some dragoon muskets in France were an exception.

Rounded collars to strengthen socket rears became well established in England on Board of Ordnance 'Land Pattern' musket bayonets. The isosceles triangular-sectioned blades, forged with rounded shanks and distinct 'shoulders', became 'hollow' on the outer faces only. Shanks were welded to the outside of the socket with a distinctive shield attachment. Rounded ledges or 'stops' at shoulders provided support in leather scabbards and sealed them from the ingress of water. This became the 'Brown Bess' bayonet. Sweden favoured some of the same features but used a wing-bolt fixing.

Some Dutch/German bayonets had an enlarged stop and facetted or lenticular-sectioned blades.

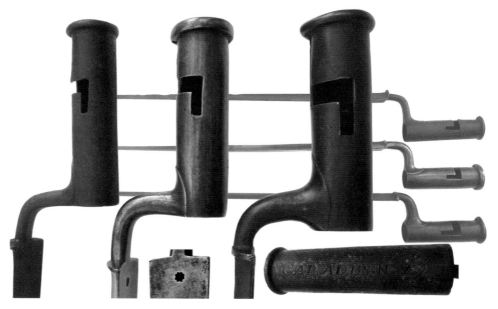

Fig. 62 Early 'Land Pattern' bayonets *c.* 1720–40 with collars, different shaped shield attachments and scabbard ledges. Left/top: The earliest marked 'Capt.Adms.N.19', rare 'Company' designation. Centre: Possible new type of 1727 from Lewisham with 'flower' smith's mark. Right/bottom: *c.* 1740 with pointed shield (Courtesy of John Humphries)

Fig. 63 Russian *Obrazets 1737* 'shtyk' fitted side-barrel stud.

Fig. 64 'Shields' and scabbard ledges from the bayonets seen at the top of this page. (John Humphries)

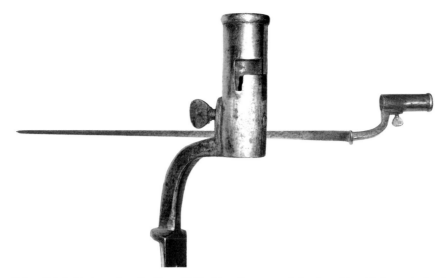

Fig. 65 Swedish *hylsbajonett* for *Musköt m/1747* with collar, squared shank, scabbard ledge and wing-bolt. Many were made at Wira Bruk. (Courtesy of Per Holmback)

Fig. 66 Strengthened scabbard ledge on Norwegian *döllebajonett m/1746*, also used on some Germanic models.

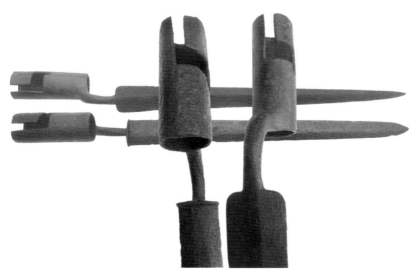

Fig. 67 'Dutch' flattened lozenge-bladed bayonets, *c.* 1730–63, to fit top and bottom barrel studs. These were still used by European troops in North America during the Seven Years War (1756–63).

Shanks from Austria, German states and Russia were often squared. Frequently, countries extended the outer fullers of their triangular-sectioned blades, without a ledge, into the shank. Sweden, Norway, Denmark, Saxony and Prussia were sometimes exceptions.

Engraved decorative lines around fronts and rears of tubes, or inverted 'Vs' above shank bases, were typical Saxon, Prussian and French characteristics.

Fig. 68 Child's bayonet from Schloss Dyck, Cologne, *c.* 1750. Typical squared shank and recurved blade shoulders.

Fig. 69 Outer fullered blade shoulders on French *baïonnette modèle 1763*, compared with English 'Land Pattern' ledge.

Fig. 70 Prussian *dillenbajonett* with engraved lines around socket, from around 1750. Markings on shank are museum alpha-numerics. (Courtesy of Jeff Hayes)

Fixing Systems to 1818

From the late seventeenth century until today, the method by which the socket bayonet was fitted to a firearm has taxed the most ingenious of minds. Originally, hand manufacture was incapable of making a consistent fit between musket barrel and socket. A requirement for blade attachment during combat with shot and pike usage exacerbated the problem. The initial form of split-socket, with simple notch for the barrel foresight, allowed adjustment of bore size but was inherently weak. Designers closed the tube seam for strength but then had to allow for 'slop' between components. Insecure bayonets during musket fire or hand-to-hand fighting were not desirable!

Several basic approaches were attempted. The tube mortise, plus the number or position of the barrel studs, was varied. Sometimes a leaf spring or clip/hook was added to the socket or firelock to engage a stud or opening on the bayonet. Rotational socket bands or clasps ('locking rings') with openings for the sight/stud and wing-bolts to grip the musket barrel appeared. Combinations were employed. Rarely a permanently attached 'socket' with spring-operated blade also served.

A two-step slot was often the primary fixation method. The source of the mortise was important as friction and the weight of the blade, through gravity, held the bayonet in place. Blades aligned to the right side of the firelocks' foresights had the initial socket opening behind the shank, but 180 degrees beyond when used with sub-barrel studs. Third legs improved security and sometimes twin bosses on barrels required two opposed mortises. Use of extra slots, as used in Saxony, often introduced spring clips on musket forends to prevent socket rotation. Bayonet rims were then notched. The United States of America's Springfield Armory (1783) introduced a 'T' mortise in August 1813.

Fig. 71 Knights of St John split-socket bayonet with simple 'notch' cut from open seam. (Courtesy of Palace Armoury, Grand Master's Palace, Valletta, Malta)

Fig. 72 Under-barrel French *modèle 1763* (left) and foresight fitted *modèle 1728* (right). Notice where mortise begins.

Fig. 73 Lieutenant Joseph Gillmore's experimental musket bayonet made by Messrs. Forsyth & Co., London 1815. Both foresight and sub-barrel stud, so two mortises on socket.

Fig. 74 Under-muzzle bayonet hook on Brunswick musket. (Courtesy of Shawn Gibson)

Fig. 75 United States Model 1812 bayonet with added bridge and 'T' mortise.

Austria refined under-barrel hook systems for the *gewehre M.1767, 1774* and *1784*. Zig-zag mortises combined with holes near the rim for clips. Upper and lower barrel studs were used. France's *baïonnette modèle 1774* followed, but the hook engaged a basal collar. Austria's *stichbajonett M.1799* and Prussia's *dillenbajonett Modell 1809* extended the principle with cammed sockets.

Fig. 76 On the left, an Austrian *stichbajonett M.1799,* and to the right a Prussian *dillenbajonett Modell 1809* with cammed sockets and no slots. In the centre is a Rimmed French *baïonnette modèle 1774* with mortise.

Fig. 77 Austrian *stichbajonett gewehre M.1767, 1774* & *1784* with holes for under-barrel musket clips. Two later models used foresight studs. Notice the armourer's mark.

Britain favoured external leaf springs on some Brown Bess variants. Spring tips were thickened to lock behind sights. Prototypes were followed by the United East India Company's 1771 'Windus's Pattern' and Ezekial Baker's 1818 'Improved' model. Springs were attached to collars. Denmark reversed this position with Christian Wilken Kyhl's 1794 muzzle-bolted version. Eared springs enclosed studs. *Musköt m/1794* and later types from Denmark and Norway used the design. In 1772 John Hirst of London was paid for '… fitting Springs and altering the Bayonets of 600 Long Land Musquet[s].'

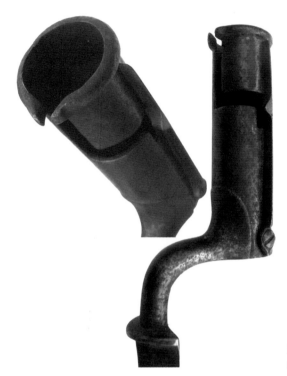

Fig. 78 English 'colonel's pattern' bayonet with side-acting leaf spring on socket, *c.* 1720.

Fig. 79 United East India Company's 'Windus's Pattern' (left) and 'Baker's Improved Pattern' (right). The 1771–1803 design had a shorter spring than the 1818 model.

These may have been lateral springs ninety degrees to the socket bore. England's 'New Land Pattern' musket simplified this form in 1802.

France's *baïonnette pour fusil de soldat modèle 1768* introduced a locking ring adjacent to the socket's rear collar, with a single mortise for the foresight. The clasp slot was 180 degrees from the fastening bolt. A round socket pin acted as bearing surface. Two years later, the stud was moved below the muzzle. General Huth of Denmark's *infanterigevaer model 1785* adopted a hinged ring set into a slot. Under-barrel stud models were similar in 1789 and 1791. Hanover's *Alt-Hannoversches Infanteriegewehr M/1773* used broad solid rings with concealed interior pins and 't' socket slots to allow limited rotation. England's 1794 Duke of Richmond's musket pattern and 'Infantry Rifle' of 1815 copied this style.

Fig. 80 Christian Wilken Kyhl's spring on Danish *Musköt m/1794* bayonet. On the right is the English 1802 'New Land Pattern'.

Fig. 81 'Land Pattern' bayonets with lateral springs, probably converted by John Hirst in 1772. Markings indicate 'D' and 'H' companies with weapon numbers '26' and '34'. (Courtesy Jeff Hayes and Shawn Gibson)

Fig. 82 Basal locking rings of French *baïonnette pour fusil de soldat modèle 1768* and *1771. 1771* ring-fitted sub-barrel tenon. Shown open and closed. (Courtesy of Pierre Renoux and Author's Collection)

Fig. 83 Danish bayonet for *infanterigevaer model 1785* with hinged ring and pin in a slot. (Courtesy of Per Holmback)

Fig. 84 To the left, basal locking ring of *Alt-Hannoversches Infanteriegewehr M/1773* with 't' slot and internal stud on socket. At the top of the image, an English 'Duke of Richmond's Musket' pattern 1794. To the right, a reverse mortised Baker 'infantry rifle', 1815.

France's *baïonnette modèle 1777* made the biggest design improvement with a clasp on the middle part of the socket. Locking rings, collared above, pinned below and combined with three-step slots, were copied by numerous European nations.

Wing-bolts were mainly Swedish features. Main drawbacks were easy loss and the risk of over-tightening into musket bores. From 1696 until 1791, bolts moved from the socket sides, base of the shank and eventually to flanges that connected the foresight, not the barrel. Austria and England used bolts on Giuseppe Crespi of Milan's 1770 carbine and Durs Egg's 1786 experimental dragoon models. North American artisans also imitated the device.

Late eighteenth-century England explored some permanently attached bayonets folded from the side of the barrel. These were more successful on pistols and musketoons.

Fig. 85 French *baïonnette modèle 1777* with three-step slot and clasp in the middle of socket. Many nations copied this style.

Fig. 86 Swedish wing-bolts on bayonets for (left) *Musköts m/1762* and (right) *1799*. The later design fitted a sight stud.

Fig. 87 Wing-bolt with set-screw used on Durs Egg's 1786 experimental dragoon spear bayonet. From volunteer carbine spear bayonet by Gully.

Halcyon Years – Eighteenth and Early Nineteenth Centuries

For over a hundred years, the socket bayonet became significant at 'set-piece' actions in Europe and elsewhere. Although artillery and musket fire, plus disease, were the main killers on the battlefield, the deployment of lightly armed 'spearmen' altered tactics considerably. Massed smooth-bored musketry was only effective at shorter ranges. Manuals of exercise and treatise of military discipline developed to control firelocks with bayonets, synchronise firepower, and move men into column, line or square as circumstances changed. Different nations decided that two or three ranks provided the most efficient arrangements. Emphasis was placed on anti-cavalry defence. Slow-to-load firearms wielders were vulnerable once muskets were discharged. With bayonets fitted, horses would not charge massed soldiers. Tacticians soon realised the aggressive potential of the arm. Volley or platoon discharges decimated opponents until bayonet assaults concluded an action. British troops developed a reputation for rigid discipline under attack, superb synchronised musket fire and fearless skill with the bayonet. Casualties inflicted by blades were normally insignificant but psychological effects won the day.

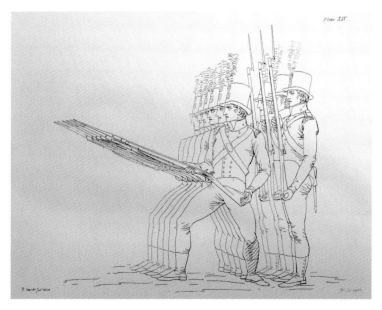

Fig. 88 Royal Marines' musket fencing system proposed by Robert Torrens to Col. Butler, 30 September 1817. (Courtesy of C. Gray, RMAS Archives)

Bright uniforms, flying colours and formal movements of infantry, artillery and cavalry became common. The Wars of the Spanish and Austrian Succession (1702–13 & 1742–48), Seven Years War (1756–63), War of American Independence (1775–83), French Revolutionary War (1793–1801) and Napoleonic War (1803–15) were typical. At the Battle of Culloden, 16 April 1746, the 'Highland charge' was broken when each government soldier bayonet-thrusted into the armpit of the Scotsman on his right (as he raised his sword) and so avoided blade deflection from targes on the left arms of the adversaries ahead. At the siege of Toulon, 17 December 1793, Capitaine Napoleon Bonaparte was stabbed in the thigh by a sergeant of the 18th (Royal Irish) Regiment with a bayonet. History might have changed forever!

Irregular warfare with rifles threatened the pre-eminence of the musket and bayonet in North America. Thick vegetation aided the guerrilla tactics employed by Native Americans and rebels against British 'Redcoats'. Captured, donated and homemade socket bayonets helped rebellious American colonists match the discipline of King George III's troops. Thus independence was achieved on 3 September 1783.

In India, the bayonet piece remained 'queen of the battlefield' until the mid-nineteenth century. Poorly armed, and led, opponents were outfought by United East India Company European-style presidency armies. Africa and Asia experienced similar for many decades.

Demand for bayonets stimulated advanced manufacturing techniques. Basic designs were standardised so that larger armies, for example the French and British during the Napoleonic War, received the most efficient (and economical) weapons. Specialist artillery, cadet, cavalry, and dragoon branches of armies developed individual carbines. Naval forces required bayonets for boarding and landing operations.

Fig. 89 The Battle of Culloden, 16 April 1746. The 'Highland charge' is seen in the centre. (Originally printed in *British Battles on Land and Sea, Vol. 2*, 1897)

Fig. 90 British Ferguson breech-loaded flintlock rifle by Durs Egg. Saw action at Brandywine Creek, North America, 1777. (Courtesy of the Trustees Weapons Collection, Land Warfare Centre, Warminster)

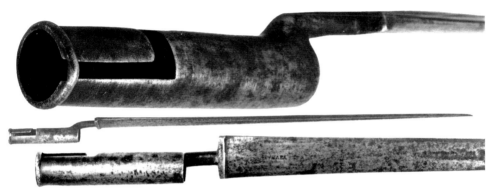

Fig. 91 Ferguson bayonet by Samuel Harvey. Short shank as the rifle was breech-loaded. (Courtesy of Brian Cavill)

Fig. 92 American 'blacksmith' socket bayonets made for Brown Bess and Charleville muskets in around 1780. Crude technology. Note the double mortise.

Socket Bayonets

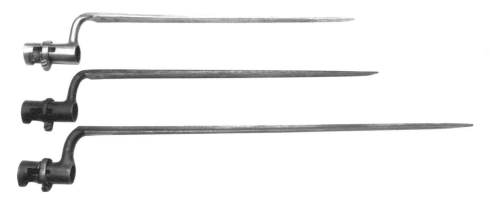

Fig. 93 French socket bayonets. Top to bottom: *baïonnette mle. 1777*, *mle. 1777 corrigé AN IX* and *mle. AN IX à lame de 19 pouces* (used on *mousqueton de cavalerie mle. AN IX*).

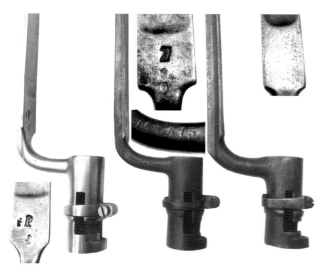

Fig. 94 Another look at the bayonets in the previous image. Note the similar median locking rings, arsenal and view markings on blades and issue inscription on shank.

Fig. 95 Evolution of Brown Bess. Left to right: 'Long Land' (1740–1760), 'Short Land' (1750–1768) and 'India Pattern' (1797–1816).

Fig. 96 The same sockets as the previous image. The shield was removed from 'Long Land' around 1740. Viewer '5' marked early 'Short Land', but forty-six inspectors were working by 1816. Maker's name and Board of Ordnance marking '295' is Swedish.

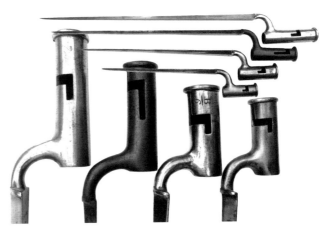

Fig. 97 British carbine bayonets. Top to bottom: 'Light Dragoon' *c.* 1756 (or 'Light Infantry Fusil' *c.* 1755); 'Artillery & Highlanders' *c.* 1755; 'Elliott's Carbine' *c.* 1773, and 'Cadet Carbine' *c.* 1773 (possibly produced by the Royal Military Academy, Woolwich). The 'Cadet Carbine' used smaller calibres than the musket bore of 0.75 inch.

Fig. 98 British volunteer rifle sword-socket bayonet from around 1790, at least 18 made. The bladed rifle barrel foresight was very narrow.

Fig. 99 Austrian bayonets. Two have typical quadrangular blades. Left to right: *Stitchbajonett M.1798, M.1799* and *Haubajonett M.1796* for *Jägerstutzen M.1796.* There are French-style locking rings on the first and last. The under-barrel spring catch on *Gewehr M.1798* was replaced by a locking ring in 1799.

Fig. 100 To the left, a Swedish *bajonett* for *Gevär m/1815* with basal locking ring. On the right, a Württemburg *c.* 1820 hinged median clasp. Note the large issue markings.

Percussion Ignition, Rifling and Breech-Loading to Mass-Production – Early Nineteenth Century

Britain's Industrial Revolution aimed technical focus at agriculture and commerce rather than warfare. A burgeoning empire from which to source raw materials, improvements with steam power, use of coal, cast iron and steel and improved maritime and canal transport did not dislodge the craft-based skills of gunsmiths and bayonet makers for a century. The emergent United States of America had abundant resources, but lacked skilled manpower. Attempts to create products with less labour stimulated machine innovations and led to mass-production. Entrepreneurs like Eli Whitney (1765–1825) focused on the textile industry. The 'cotton gin' patent (14 March 1794) presaged interchangeable components and the 'Armoury' or 'American system of manufacturing'. Captain John Hancock Hall (1781–1841) and Simeon North (1765–1852) implemented the military aspects of the idea. The former's 'US Rifle, Model 1819' breech-loaded rifle bayonet was the first to be fully standardised. Derived from the 'T' mortise 'US Musket, Model 1816', or 'M.1822', bayonet, it foreshadowed the weapon's eventual decline. North's milling machine worked with Hall displaced hand-filing and allowed accurately shaped parts to interchange.

Fig. 101 Left: Offset sight-bridge of 'US Rifle, Model 1819' (Hall) breech-loading rifle bayonet. Right: 'US Musket, Model 1816'. Both with 'T' mortise.

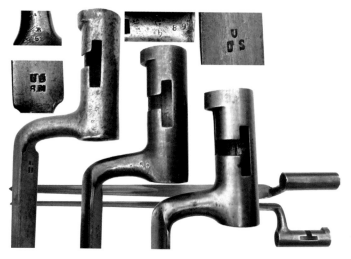

Fig. 102 On the left, a 'US Musket, Model 1816', in the centre, a 'Model 1822', and on the right, a 'US Rifle, Model 1819'. The 'SM' stands for Springfield Manufacturing Co. and the 'U' for John Unseld. Alpha-numerical series markings.

Elsewhere, the glut of ex-Napoleonic War large-calibre flintlocks delayed the implementation of percussion ignition (fulminate) developments by Rev. Alexander Forsyth (1768–1843), Joseph Manton (1766–1835) and Joshua Shaw (1776–1860) until the 1840s. Conservative thinkers in Austria, England, France, Sweden and the USA retrofitted muskets with 'tube', 'pill' or 'cap' primed locks. Bayonets remained unchanged. France's 0.71-inch (17.5-mm) calibre flintlock *fusil d'infanterie modèle 1822* became a percussioned *mle.1822-1840 transformée*. The bayonet was similar to the *modèle 1777/AN IX* except for an extended blade length. Other nations imitated this, for example the USA's 'Musket, Model 1835'. Liège, in independent Belgium (1830), specialised in imitations of French models for smaller European states such as Switzerland. Russia cloned the weapons. In the 1830s, England 'product improved' the 'India Pattern' musket in its new Royal Small Arms Manufactory at Enfield Lock, London, which had begun in 1814. Bayonets gained an under-barrel catch system based on 'Hanoverian' originals. A better spring, designed by Inspector of Small Arms George Lovell (1788–1854), appeared in 1844. Parallel models were used by the United East India Company.

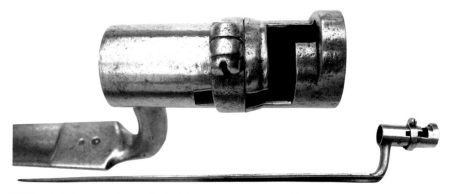

Fig. 103 French *baïonnette mle.1822* for *fusil d'infanterie modèle 1822*. The 416-mm blade was extended from the AN IX.

Fig. 104 On the left, French *baïonnette mle.1822*, and, on the right, *baïonnette mle.1822 N* with a larger bore for 18-mm calibre. Socket marked 'N' over 'T' for 'nouveau' and 'Tulle' (factory).

Fig. 105 Left: 'US Musket, Model 1822'. Right: 'Model 1835' copy of French *baïonnette mle.1822*.

Fig. 106 From bottom-left to top-right: 'US Musket, Model 1835'; Russian 'shtyk' *Obrazets 1828*; Swiss *Gewehre Ordonnanz 1817-67 Infanterie*; French *modèle 1822*; Belgian *modèle 1841*. Below: United States ownership 'US'; Belgian blade maker 'LJ'; Swiss 'Zaughaus (arsenal) Zürich (weapon) 1539'; Russian 'hammer' Tula arsenal and smith's stamp; Belgian 'B-F' Beuret Frères, Liège.

Fig. 107 Left and right: Final 'India Pattern' *c.* 1803. In the centre is 'New Pattern Lovell's Percussion Musket' from around 1839. Samuel Dawes made 'India Pattern' bayonets to 1805. Note the blade shoulders. The long mortise slot may be for a Baker Rifle.

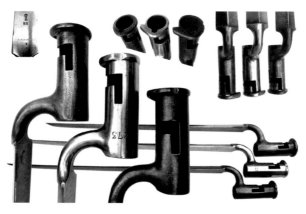

Fig. 108 From bottom-left to top-right: 'New Pattern Lovell's Percussion Musket' *c.* 1839; 'Lovell's Percussion Musket' *c.* 1844; 'Pattern 1851 rifle-musket'. The pattern 1838, 1839 and 1842 muskets used the Hanoverian catch (plain collar) until Lovell's catch of 1844. The P.1839 musket lacked back-sight so un-notched collar. 'EX' is 'Extra Service'.

Fig. 109 Top: 'New Pattern Lovell's Percussion Musket', *c.* 1839. Bottom: United East India Company 'Type E' with 'flat' on collar, *c.* 1842. Both used the Hanoverian catch. In the centre is a 'Type F' from around 1845, which had a flange with hole for barbed musket spring.

After 1835, Austria converted *Infanteriegewehr Modell 1798* flint muskets to Giuseppe Console's tube-lock system. In 1840, an improved lock by Vinzenz Baron von Augustin (1780–1859) became the *M.1840*. From 1845, he supervised the construction of a Vienna state arsenal. New percussion muskets 1840 and 1842 included a post-1838 bayonet catch. Similar to the *stitchbajonett M.1799*, it had a straight mortise for the musket's barbed under-barrel spring. The *Haubajonett M.1849* for *Jägerstutzen M.1849* combined a basal locking-ring and lengthened three-step mortise with twin barrel lugs for security.

A Prussian successor to the *dillenbajonett Modell 1839* surprised the world, fitted to the first bolt-action needle-rifle. Johann Nicolaus Dreyse's (1787–1867) *Leichte Percussionsgewehr Modell 1841 (Zündnadelgewehr)* was made at Gewehrfabrik Potsdam-Spandau, Saarn and Danzig. Obturation problems limited its success as an export weapon. Bayonets had single sub-barrel mortises with French 1770s-style basal clasps. Recesses above bolt terminals clipped over clearing rods to prevent rotation.

Sweden's modernised percussion *gevär m/1840* and *m/1845* continued with basal locking ring bayonets. The Norwegian Army adopted a very advanced '18-lödig' *kammerlader gevær M/1842* after 18 May 1842. The Khyl spring catch, fullered triangular-bladed *døllebayonett* had a basal locking ring after 23 September 1844.

Fig. 110 Left: Austrian *stitchbajonett M.1799* for barbed musket spring. Right: *Haubajonett M.1849* for *Jägerstutzen M.1849*.

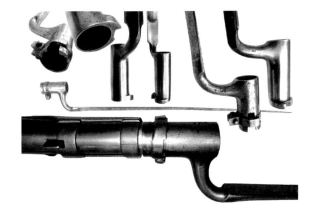

Fig. 111 Left and below: Prussian *dillenbajonett Modell 1841* for Zündnadelgewehr. Centre: *Modell 1839*. The latter used a musket spring catch.

Fig. 112 Swedish *hylsbajonett m/1840* for *gevär m/1840* and *m/1845*. Issued to the 9th Regiment, 7th Company – bayonet number '986'.

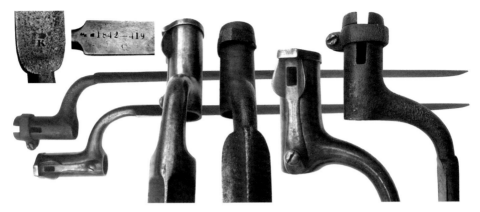

Fig. 113 Top: Norwegian post-1844 *døllebayonett* with basal ring for *kammerlader gevær M/1842*. Bottom: Danish *bajonet* for *Glat infanterimusket m/1841*. Norway replaced the Khyl spring catch with basal ring. 'K' is Kongsberg Arsenal, Norway. M/1841 was issued in 1842 as weapon '419'.

Some German states, for example Bavaria, Hanover and Saxony (Oberndorf) favoured basal clasp designs but varied their blade arrangements.

In 1847, the Frenchman Claude-Étienne Minié (1804–1879), after initial work by Henri-Gustave Delvigne (1800–1876) and Louis-Étienne de Thouvenin (1791–1882), stimulated another major military innovation. Cylindro-conoidal soft-lead bullets, sometimes combined with a 'pillar breech' (*carabine à tige*), made a general issue rifle possible. The *fusil d'infanterie modèle 1842 T (transformée)* had a strengthened bayonet after 1847. The 'Minié rifle' was admired by George Lovell in England, so some muzzle-loaded 'Pattern 1851 rifle-muskets' were manufactured at Enfield Lock as the first universal English infantry rifles. The 0.702-inch (17.9-mm) calibre design, with 'Lovell's catch' bayonet, perpetuated Brown Bess technology. In 1853, a new rifle-musket, soon with interchangeable components from the 'Armoury System', raised standards to new heights. Mass production had arrived.

Fig. 114 Top right: Bavarian *dillenbajonett M/1826* for *Infanteriegewehr 'neuer Art' M/1826* (Manson). Bottom left: Saxony (Oberndorf) *M/1835* for *Infanteriegewehr M/1835*. Notice the blade differences. Inset: Saxon crown mark with issue to 12th Regiment, bayonet '181'.

Fig. 115 Hanoverian *dillenbajonett M/1854* for *Pickelgewehre 'neuen Modell' 1854*. This had a rifle spring catch and was issued to 6th Regiment ('VI'), Company 'A', as weapon '2'.

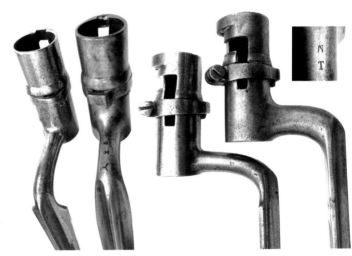

Fig. 116 Left: French *baïonnette modèle 1822* for *fusil d'infanterie mle.*1822. Right: *modèle 1822 modifiée 1847 N.* The locking ring, shank and blade shoulders were thickened. Socket mark is 'N' over 'T' for 'nouveau' and 'Tulle'.

Fig. 117 Older British bayonets used in the 1850s. Top to bottom: 'Sappers & Miners Carbine' P.1843; United East India Company 'Sappers Carbine, Pattern F' 1845; 'Irish Constabulary Carbine', P.1840. Note the knuckle-bow and blade spring.

The Height of Development and International Wars – Mid-Nineteenth Century

Although outdated, musket systems remained in service well into the nineteenth century. England created a socket bayonet in 1852 that was the summit of technological development. 'Rifle-Musquet, Pattern 1853' with 'Bayonet, Pattern 1853' set the standard for Austria, Bavaria, Spain, the USA and so on, over the next decades. Although early, 6 October 1853, bayonet orders used traditional Birmingham 'outwork' methods, the Royal Manufactory at Enfield Lock began partial mechanisation from 1855 to 1858. The London Armoury Company, founded 1856, converted in 1860. In 1854, Birmingham's traditional gunmakers formed a consortium, the Birmingham Small Arms Trade, to remain in competition. A new factory at Small Heath, opened in 1861, was automated to become Birmingham Small Arms Co. Ltd. The 1851 'American System' of Colt's pistol factory at Bessborough Place, London was influential. Imported USA machinery allowed unskilled labour, particularly women and children, to produce interchangeable parts. The economic advantage through improved rate of manufacture was of particular value to the extensive British Empire. Products served on every known continent and ocean.

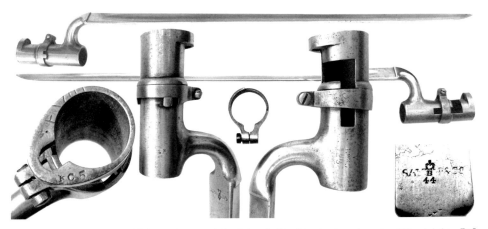

Fig. 118 'Bayonet, Pattern 1853'. An early example by Salter & Co., Birmingham, issued to Warwickshire Rifle Volunteers. The locking ring design allowed better adjustment. Inspected by Birmingham viewer '44'.

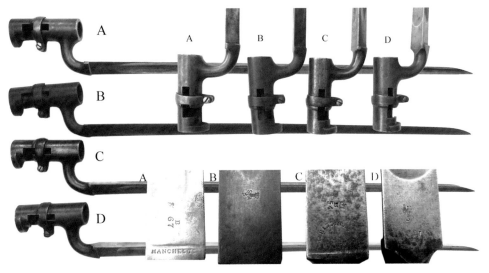

Fig. 119 Pattern 1853s. A: Manchester (possibly Francis Preston); B: Birmingham Small Arms Trade; C: W. Higgins & Sons, Birmingham; D: Interchangeable design Royal Manufactory, Enfield Lock. Note the fuller shapes of A and C.

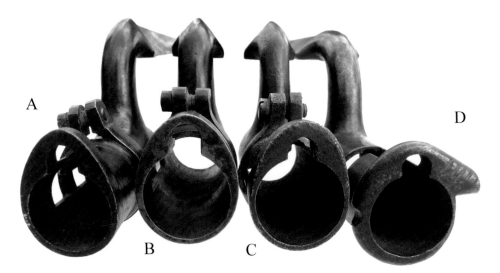

Fig. 120 A: India Government 'Musket, smooth-bore, Pattern 1859'; B: Royal Manufactory, Enfield interchangeable P.1853; C: Birmingham trade P.1853; D: 'Lovell's Percussion Musket', *c.* 1844. A and D had larger bores than P.1853s.

Inventors focused on breech-loaded rifles, but governments desired simple, reliable systems that would not waste ammunition. Single-shot, muzzle-loaded, reduced-calibre (0.577 inch) percussion lock 'Minié' rifle-muskets and carbines provided solutions. The P.1853 bayonet was ultra-modern compared with Brown Bess. The bridged socket, for foresight, had a three-step mortise and median locking-ring. The clasp bolt over the sight bridge allowed better adjustment. A robust rounded shank with scabbard ledge supported an almost equilateral sectioned fullered blade with beak point. The extra range of the weapon undermined bayonet battlefield tactics as a 'charge' now had to cover greater distances under fire.

The firearm saw three conflicts in its first decade. The Crimean War (1853–56), Indian Mutiny (1857–58) and American Civil War (1861–65) emphasised the superiority of the rifle-musket. Insufficient production capacity opened P.1853 contracts for Liège, St. Étienne and Windsor, Vermont. It being issued in the Crimea impressed French and Russian officials. An 'Indian Army' was formed after the United East India Company's failings and its abolition by the British government. Fears of another insurrection introduced smooth-bored P.1853 imitations after 1858. Indian and Nepalese enterprises cloned these. Commercial rifle-muskets reached Union and Confederate forces alike from Birmingham, Liège, London and Manchester until 'US Rifle-Muskets Model of 1855' proliferated. English weapons influenced arms technology at Springfield Armory, Massachusetts and Harper's Ferry, Virginia. Partial destruction of the latter in 1861 stimulated non-interchangeable versions via commercial organisations until Springfield could expand. Similar bayonets appeared on breech-loaders, for example Sharps after 1849 and Spencer in 1860, plus Confederate arms.

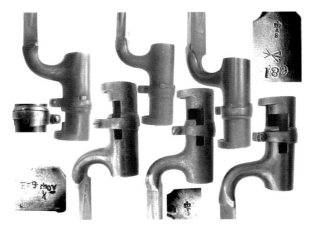

Fig. 121 British Government contract P.1853s. Left to right: Liège, Belgium (crown 'L') Felix Escoffier; St Étienne', France (crown 'F'), and Robbins & Lawrence, Windsor, Vermont, USA (crown 'A'). The Liège ones have round stop pins.

Fig. 122 India Government 'Musket, smooth-bore, Pattern 1859' bayonets from, to the left, Enfield and, to the right, Manchester. Bombay issue Sepoy '539', 12th Company, 23rd Native Infantry and Sepoy '66', 7th Co., 23rd N.I. Note the variant markings.

Fig. 123 On the left, Indian, and, on the right, Nepalese P.1853 bayonets.. Shank Nagari markings 'Number:1:4' and '632'.

Fig. 124 Top-left: bayonets for 'US Rifle-Musket Model of 1855'. The rotation of locking clasp was extended by 0.2 inches in 1863. Produced in Springfield ('S'), Amoskeag (star) and elsewhere. To the bottom right is a 'Spencer Repeating Rifle M.1860'. The bore was larger and the stop pin on the socket in a different position. 'L' viewer Samuel Leonard.

Austria's Vienna Arsenal, founded 1849, manufactured *Infanteriegewhr Modell 1854* and *Jägerstuzen M/1854* bayonets with helical slots. These saw service in the American Civil War. The Bavarian *Infanteriegewehr M/1858* was similar with a three-sided blade. Prussia adopted the median clasp on the updated *Zundnadel-Infanteriegewehre M/1862*. Spain used the P.1853 until the *Fusil Modelo 1,857 Para Infantería* had a redesigned bayonet with 'Europeanised' blade shoulders and no scabbard ledge. Production was in Spain, Birmingham, Solingen and Liège.

Fig. 125 Top-right: Austrian *Jägerstuzen M/1854*. Centre: Bavarian *Infanteriegewhr M/1858*. Bottom-left: Austrian *Infanteriegewhr Modell 1854* (Lorenz). Note the helical slots. The 'Star' signifies Vienna Arsenal and the crown 'I' was a Bavarian mark.

Fig. 126 Prussian *Zundnadel-Infanteriegewehre M/1862*, a direct imitation of English P.1853. The Gothic letters are proof markings.

Fig. 127 Spanish *bayoneta* for *Fusil Rayado Modelo 1,857 Para Infantería* from, to the top-right, Liège in Belgium; in the centre, Eibar in Spain, and in the bottom-left, Solingen, Westphalia. 'Z.Y.Compa' signifies Eibar, the crown 'O' signifies Oviedo. The 'Knight's head' signifies Carl R. Kirschbaum, Solingen. Crown 'BSTA/8' signifies Birmingham Small Arms Trade viewer '8' (the retailer).

By 1857, France had adopted brass-hilted sabre bayonets but used sockets on the 17.5- and 18-mm caliber *fusils à percussion*. *Baïonnettes à lame de 51 cm* and *51 cm N* reissued the earlier French socket with longer four-sided blades. Needle-fire bolt-actioned *fusil d'infanterie modèle 1866* used an iconic 'Chassepot' sword-bayonet, but the *gendarmerie à cheval mle.1866/74* and *1874* utilised Anglicised sockets with long quadrangular blades.

Russia's defeat in the Crimean War stimulated a rearmament process. Foreign and domestic technologies were re-examined. Indentured gunmakers slowed progress at Ishevsk, Sestrovesk and Tula. *Obrazets 1854* and *1856* rifle muskets, some bought from Birmingham and Liège, had median ring socket bayonets with rearranged mortises. Sweden's *bajonett* for *Räfflat Minégevär m/1855*, from Liège, was very similar. Local versions followed in 1857. Norway bought the *kammerladningsgevær M/1846* abroad but the *M/1860* was Norwegian. *Døllebayonetten* had basal rings and internal stud systems. After 1851, Denmark renamed the Suhl-made Schleswig Holstein *Tapriffel m/1849* as 'model 1854'. The bayonet had Khyl's spring catch.

Within fifteen years, many rifle-muskets had been converted to breech-loading, so the bayonets remained the same.

Fig. 128 Top: French *baïonnette à lame de 51 cm* for *fusil à percussion*, 1857. Note the quadrangular blade. Bottom: *Baïonnette modèle 1822–1847 N modifiée 1860*, for older rifled-up muskets – *fusil de zouave modèle 1853* and *balle de chasseurs 1860*, etc. Note the sight. Socket mark 'N' over 'S' for 'nouveau' and 'St Étienne'.

Fig. 129 Bottom-left: French *baïonnette modèle 1866 de gendarmerie à cheval* (Chassepot). Top-right: *mle. 1866/74* (Gras). Note the altered locking ring and sight opening. The 'G' stands for 'gendarmerie'.

Fig. 130 Swedish *bajonett Räfflat m/1860*, in the top-left, compared to the similar Russian *Obrazets 1856* in the bottom-right. The locking rings rotate differently.

Fig. 131 Top-right: Russian *Obrazets 1856* for *vintovka Ob.1856*. Some were made in Liège, Belgium ('JR &'), Birmingham, England (crown BSAT 7) by Birmingham Small Arms Trade, viewer '7, and, to the right, Russia. In the bottom-left is *Ob.1854* for *vintovka Ob.1854*, with a French-style clasp and sight, Russian smith's stamp and '34317' serial number.

Fig. 132 Top-left: Swedish *bajonett Räfflat m/*1860. Centre: *Wredesgevär m/1860*. Bottom-right: *Räfflat Minégevär m/1855* (flotten). Note the different sight bridge shapes and the viewer's initials on shanks. Also the serial numbers or dates. Note the 'flower' for navy (*flotten*) ownership.

Fig. 133 Top-right: *Døllebayonetten* for *kammerlader gevær M/1860*. Bottom-left: *kammerladningsgevær M/1846*. Blades differ. Basal rings have enclosed studs. Both from Kongsberg Arsenal (crown 'K').

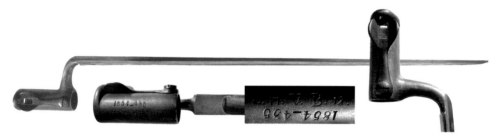

Fig. 134 Schleswig Holstein *Tapriffel m/1849* from Suhl, reissued in Denmark as *SuhlerTapriffel m/1854* with Khyl's spring catch. Schleswig Holstein 5th Battalion no.12 ('S.H.V.B.12') was replaced by the '1854' date and weapon no. '435'.

Twilight Years – Late Nineteenth Century

A five-year gap between the American Civil War and Franco-Prussian War (1870–71) meant antagonists had current weaponry and numerous surplus arms available. Advances in breech-loading, fixed ammunition, reduced calibre size and the use of magazines coincided. Such developments relegated the socket bayonet to a more secondary position. Sword and knife bayonets became status symbols for rifle-armed troops. Showy sidearms or utility knives had more appeal to military designers now troops were less likely to meet in set-piece actions. Some countries with established rifle-musket technology had colonies in Africa, Asia, Australasia and South America to police. A period of compromise to evaluate new designs, avoid an expensive re-equipment process and employ current weapons against less sophisticated foes began. Ordnance boards of Austria, Belgium, Britain, France, Scandinavia, Spain, Switzerland, Russia, Turkey, USA etc. began to retrofit breech mechanisms to stored rifle-muskets as their committees deliberated. These did not need new bayonets.

Eventually, certain mechanisms, many single-shot, gained favour. Those of Augusto Albini (Italy/Belgium), Edouard de Beaumont (Holland), Hiram Berdan (Russia), Salvatore Carcano (Italy), Benjamin B. Hotchkiss (USA), James Paris Lee (Britain/USA), Jacob Jarmann (Norway/Sweden), Friedrich von Martini (Britain/Switzerland), Ferdinand Ritter von Mannlicher (Austria), Peter Paul Mauser (Germany), Sergei Ivanovich Mosin (Russia), Léon Nagant (Russia), Henry Peabody (Switzerland/Turkey/USA), E. Remington & Sons (Americas/ Sweden/Spain/USA), Friedrich Vetterli (Italy/Switzerland) and Oliver Winchester (France/Russia/Turkey/USA) surfaced.

Fig. 135 English Westley Richards rifle bayonet *c.* 1860. A breech-loaded weapon allowed shankless design (no rammer). Produced by Charles Reeves & Co., Birmingham.

Fig. 136 Austrian *stitchbajonett Extra-Corps-Gewehre Modell 1867*, with smaller socket bore.

Fig. 137 Belgian bayonets. Top-left: *fusil d'infanterie mle.1867* (system Albini-Braendlin). Bottom-right: *mle.1777-1867*, converted from *baïonnette mle.1841*. Note the fuller and bridge differences. The letters indicated regiments. 'Q' was *3e régiment de chasseurs à pied*.

Fig. 138 Bottom-centre: Dutch *baïonnettes* for *fusil d'infanterie Beaumont mle.1871* and *mle.1873* for *Sappeurkarabijn Remington mle.1870*. Two-part locking ring with twin bolts for second model. Note the issue markings and proof stamps.

Fig. 139 Top-centre: Russian 'schtyk' for *vintovka Berdana 1870* (Berdan II). *Centre-left: 1868* (Berdan I). These had different mechanisms. The bayonets were for side-barrel studs except for the dragoon version on the right. Boss lined up with clearing rod and formed 'monopod' when detached.

Some rifles abandoned the socket bayonet and others adapted older models to reduce the expense. Larger socket diameters were reduced by means of 'bushing', cutting and rewelding, or 'cold-pressing'. A mechanical press system from Lt-Col. J. B. Benton of Springfield Armory altered the 'US Bayonet, Model 1855' into the M.1873.

Sub-muzzle clearing rods were sometimes abandoned on newly manufactured small-calibre breech-loaded arms. A more accurate thrust with the bayonet in this location was possible. Median locking-ring sockets repositioned the mortise to achieve this. Britain modified P.1876 bayonets in 1895. Four-sided blade profiles, not triangular, were popular. Shorter firearms gained longer bayonets to maintain 'reach'. These were now mass-produced on interchangeable principles. Sweden upgraded the *Remingtongevär m/1867 bajonnett* to a unique press-stud catch in 1889. Imperial Russia retained the traditional socket bayonet. The 'schtyk' for the magazine-fed *trehlinejnaja vintovka obrasca 1891 goda* had a shankless quadrangular blade and unbridged socket. This was an economic necessity for the enormous Russian forces, so socket bayonet designs remained current in the twentieth century.

Despite long-range firepower, multi-shot rifles and the machine-gun which displaced the bayonet from its defensive role, there were mixed results in Britain's 'small wars'. At Isandhlwana, on 22 January 1879, troops mainly armed with the bushed Pattern 1853 bayonet and Martini-Henry rifle were slaughtered by Zulu *impis*. Hours later, the P.1876 'lunger' fulfilled its role with some success at Rorke's Drift. Tactics, not technology, determined how the weapon was to serve in future wars.

Fig. 140 Centre-left: British 'Bayonet, Rifle, breech-loading, Martini-Henry Mk I', 1872. Bushed P.1853 with an Enfield conversion marking of November 1873. Also, 'Bayonet, common, complete with locking ring, long' (P.1876) for the Martini-Henry. P.1853's locking ring was reused, hence the raised belt around socket. Produced by Birmingham Small Arms & Metal Co. and Enfield.

Fig. 141 Bottom-left: Cold-pressed 'US Bayonet, Model 1873' made from M.1855. 'A' added after adaption. Top-right: Newly made Hotchkiss M.1883 and Winchester M.1894 rifle, which were similar. Note the waisted shank.

Fig. 142 Swedish *bajonnett Jarmanngevär m/1881* with under-barrel blade. (Courtesy of Per Holmback)

Fig. 143 British 'Bayonet, Martini-Enfield/L/triangular, converted from Martini-Henry long' (P.1895). 50 per cent of the socket was replaced to realign the mortise. Note the filled slot. Enfield converted most from September 1900, along with Wilkinson Sword Co.

Fig. 144 Cruder, Egyptian Army, converted P.1876 for the Martini-Enfield rifle. Socket bushed, bridge cut and higher locking ring added. Arabic numerals.

Fig. 145 Turkish Peabody-Martini bayonet made by Providence Tool Co. USA in around 1873. 'C' view marking.

Fig. 146 Remington 'Military Breech Loading Rifle' bayonets used by many countries, such as Sweden and Spain in around 1867. Top-left: Swedish *m/1867* from Husqvarna ('H'), Carl Gustav (crown/C) factories and USA ('TN' viewer Timar Nordstrom). With 'Flotten' and 20th Rifle Battalion marks. Centre: Belgian contract. Bottom-right: Spain or Papal states with long blade.

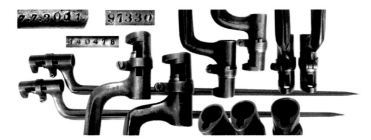

Fig. 147 Bottom-left: Swiss *stichbajonett Ordonnanz 1863*. Top-right: *1871* used on *Infanteriegewehr Ord.1863* and *Vetterli Ord.1869/71*. The sight opening was changed in 1877. 'Z.Z.' stands for Zeughaus Zurich.

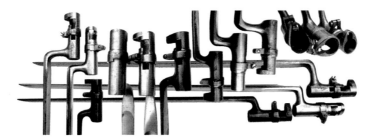

Fig. 148 Winchester used triangular blades. Top-left: Model 1894. Centre: M.1873. Bottom-right: M.1866 military 'muskets'. These were mainly commercial weapons.

Fig. 149 Remington-type triangular blades. Top: Peabody 'Army'. Centre-right: two US 'generic' designs, long and short. Bottom-left: Spanish Modelo 1,871 made under licence with different blade shoulders. 'H' viewer H. S. Hill or P. N. B. Harens from New York National Guard, contract 1872.

Fig. 150 Left: New York National Guard Remington. Right: Peabody 'Army Rifle', *c.* 1862. Note the different mortises and fullers.

Fig. 151 Coil spring catch modified Swedish *bajonnett Remingtongevär m/1867* for 8-mm calibre *gevär m/1867-89*. Converted Carl Gustav (crown/C) factory. Unique bayonet fixing. The viewers' initials can be seen.

Fig. 152 'Schtyk' for Russian *trehlinejnaja vintovka obrasca 1891 goda* (Mosin Nagant). The three-step mortise rotation changed ninety degrees to thirty degrees by 1894. Made by Ishevsk (bow & arrow), Tula (hammer) and Sestrojevsk (arrow), plus France and USA. The tip was a screwdriver.

World Wars – 1914 to 1945

By the Second Anglo Boer War (1899–1902) most major military powers, except Russia, had adopted knife or sword bayonets for bolt-action, magazine-fed rifles. Better accuracy and longer ranges relegated the bayonet to secondary role usage as a utility tool, last-ditch defence or prisoner deterrent. Outdated tactics, i.e. the bayonet attack, persisted among the officer class but drills with cold steel were intended to promote combat aggression and physical fitness in the ranks.

The First World War's (1914–18) heavy artillery, machine guns, armoured vehicles, aircraft, poisonous gas and trench warfare mainly assigned the socket bayonet to rear echelon roles. Russia's *trehlinejnaja vintovka obrasca 1891 goda* continued to serve on the Eastern Front. Production difficulties ensured the USA manufactured huge quantities after 1915. Finland obtained some – even a wire-cutter type appeared. Germany and Austria manufactured ersatz socket bayonets to equip captured Russian rifles. A global shortage of firearms ensured that obsolete rifles served in local defence and prison guard situations.

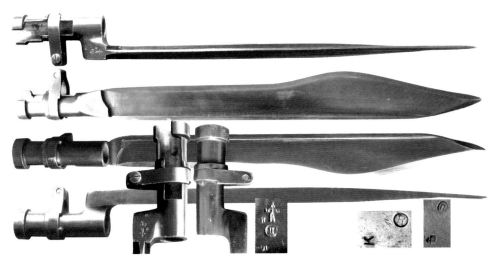

Fig. 153 Russian engineering unit trials wire-cutter bayonet, *c.* 1912–1914. Another device was attached. Made by Ishevsk (bow & arrow). Adjacent are Remington and Westinghouse symbols used on US-made *Ob.1891* bayonets (Courtesy of Krzysztof Cieciura).

Fig. 154 German *aushilfsseitengewehren* for captured Russian *trehlinejnaja vintovka obrasca 1891 goda, c.* 1915. Fullered and flat blades. The knurled sleeve locked the socket to the barrel. Note proof markings. (Courtesy of Christian Méry)

Fig. 155 Top-left: Austrian *ersatzbajonetten* for captured Russian *trehlinejnaja vintovka obrasca 1891 goda*. Bottom-right: *Repetierkarabiner Mannlicher M.1890, c.* 1915. Note the straight mortises. 'E.A.IX' stands for '*Erzeugungs Abteilung 9*' (Production Department 9).

When 'the war to end war' was over and politicians tried to negotiate a settlement for lasting peace, national bias or vested interests and social disquiet, which stimulated communism and National Socialism, doomed the process. In 1921, Britain's War Office established a Small Arms Committee to formulate a 'New Design of Rifle'. Due to the shortcomings of issue sword-bayonets in trench warfare, a diminutive 'spike' design appeared between 1925 and 1933. Its socket featured a coil-spring activated plunger catch. Prototype variants were investigated, so the 'No.4 Mark I' arrived in 1931. Troop trial quantities were manufactured at Enfield Lock.

In 1922, the Soviet 'Republic Revolutionary Military Council' sought to upgrade the Red Army's rifle. Design improvements and experimental bayonets revamped the Mosin-Nagant and the *Vintovka obrazetza 1891/30 goda* appeared on 28 April 1930. Evgeniy A. Kabakov and Irinárj Andreevich Komaritskiys' rifle kept the basic 1891 'schtyk' without locking ring but with Colonel P. K. Panshin's No.4 type plunger catch. Early Dragoon rifle versions had a shroud on the socket.

As Britain entered the Second World War (1939–45), on 3 September 1939, the 'Rifle, No.4 Mk I' and bayonet had not been manufactured in quantity. Frantic efforts

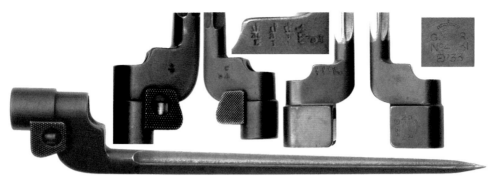

Fig. 156 British 'Bayonet, No.1 Mk II Patt.'26" trials model with catch variations. 'No.2 Mk II' dated 1931 and 'No.4 Mk I' from 1933 (Courtesy of John Humphries)

Fig. 157 Soviet Russian 'schtyk' for *vintovka obrazetza 1891/30 goda.* With Panshin sight hood and spring catches. 'Star' (right) for Tula and 'triangle/arrow' (centre-left) for Sestrojevsk arsenals.

created or modified factories to make up the shortfall. Losses at Dunkirk in May/June 1940, material shortages, threat of invasion and dangers from aerial attack altered designs. On 13 February 1941, the 'Bayonet, No.4 Mk I' (by Singer Manufacturing Co.) was replaced by a simplified 'No.4 Mk II' (rounded spike) or 'No.4 Mk II*' (two-piece body) from dispersed UK organisations, plus Canada and the USA. An even cruder 'fabricated' 'No.4 Mk III', from 12 February 1943, appeared for D-Day. High quality, experimental and crude issue models for sub-machine carbines, e.g. 'Bayonet, Sten 9-mm, Machine Carbine, Mk I' were produced.

Potential jungle warfare in the Pacific theatre, versus Japanese forces, promoted knife-bladed socket bayonets. 'Bayonet, No.7 Mk.1/L/.' for 'Carbine, Machine, Sten 9-mm, Mk V' appeared in early 1945. In 1942, Australia's 'Owen 9-mm Machine Carbine, Mk II' gained a prototype model from Lysaght of Port Kembla.

Soviet forces utilised locally manufactured knife-bladed socket bayonets during the Siege of Leningrad, which took place from 1941 to 1944.

The inexpensive socket bayonet had a new lease of life.

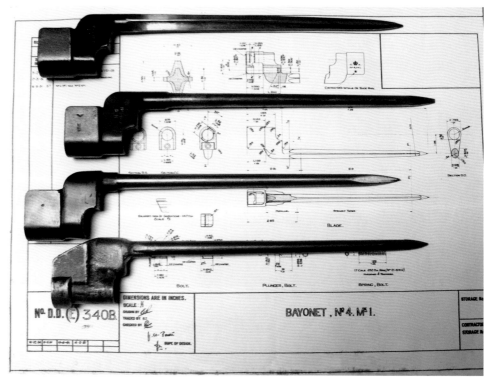

Fig. 158 Top to bottom: British 'Bayonet, No.4 Mk I' (Singer Manufacturing Co.); 'No.4 Mk II' (Singer Manufacturing Co.); 'No.4 Mk II*' (Prince-Smith & Stells Ltd); 'No.4 Mk III' (Joseph Lucas Ltd).

Fig. 159 Left to right: 'Bayonet, No.1 Mk II Patt.'26', 'Bayonet, No.4 Mk I', 'No.4 Mk II', 'No.4 Mk II*', 'No.4 Mk III'. Inset markings, left to right: 'S.M.' (Singer Manufacturing Co.), 'LB' (Longbranch, Canada), '[S]' (J. Stevens, USA), 'P.S.K.' (Prince-Smith & Stells Ltd), 'M/158' (Joseph Lucas Ltd).

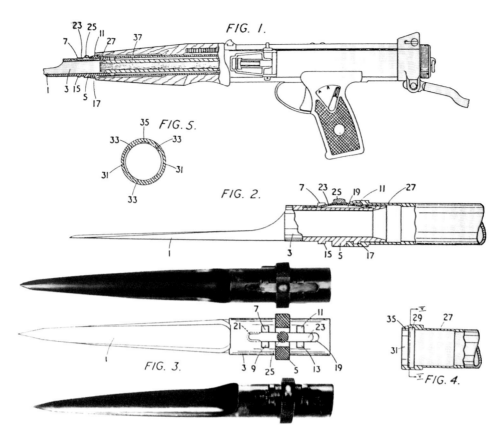

Fig. 160 Experimental 'Birmingham Small Arms Co. 9-mm Machine Carbine' and bayonet. (Patent 601,521, 6 April 1945, and Weller & Dufty Sale no.11138 1971)

Fig. 161 Experimental bayonet for 'Sub-Machine Gun V-42, Calibre 9 mm' by Joseph Veseley, 1942 (Courtesy of John Humphries)

Fig. 162 British 'Bayonet, Sten, 9-mm. Machine Carbine, Mk I' from 'Sten, Mk II'. Some with fillet welds. '1' on spike at the point of taper. B. J. Sippel Ltd marked springs and sockets.

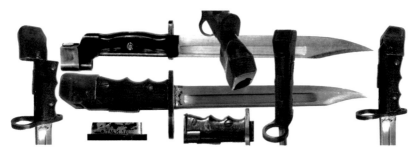

Fig. 163 Swivel socket 'Bayonet, No.7 Mk.1/L/.' for 'Carbine, Machine, Sten 9-mm., Mk V' with, at the top of the image, a prototype by Wilkinson Sword Co. Ltd produced in early 1944. Red tufnel and black plastic grips. (Courtesy of Robert Wilkinson-Latham and Author's Collection)

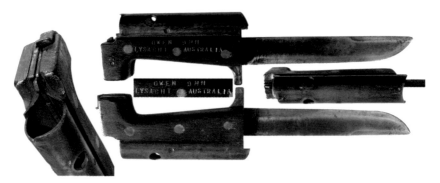

Fig. 164 Australian experimental bayonet for 'Owen 9-mm. Machine Carbine, Mk II' by Gerard Wardell, Lysaght, Port Kembla, 1942.

Fig. 165 Relic Soviet knife bladed 'blokadnik' for *vintovka obrazetza 1891/30 goda*, from the Siege of Leningrad, 1941–1944. Different blade styles appeared.

The Cold War and Beyond – 1947 to Present

Global devastation and the advent of nuclear armaments did not displace new small arms when Eastern (Soviet) and Western (US/NATO) blocs postured during the Cold War *c.* 1947–1991. Actual conflicts – the Korean War (1950–1953) and Vietnam War (1955–1975) – together with post-colonial emergencies, such as Malaya (1948–1960), Congo (1960–1964) and the Falklands (1982) used old and new weapons. Advances in metallurgy, synthetic materials, propellants and the rapid development of mechanised warfare, created handier, lighter, small-calibre, automatically operated 'assault rifles'. Most favoured a utility knife over a socket bayonet.

Britain used 'Rifle, No.4 Mk.2' and 'Carbine Machine, Sten 9-mm, Mk.5' well into the 1950s. Both received a knife-bladed 'Bayonet, No.9 Mk.1/L' after 1949. This was adopted by Pakistan and South Africa. Eire utilised some on 'Model 45 Carl Gustav Machine Carbines'. South Africa developed an unfullered 'Bayonet, Rifle, 7,70-mm (No.4 Mk.1)' in the 1960s. In 1948, Italy improvised a *Baionetta modificata compl. di fodero pe Enfield n.4* from the Modello 1891 blade and No.4 socket.

Britain's bolt-action rifle replacement was anticipated by the 'Small Arms Ideal Calibre Panel' in 1945. The project formed the 'Enfield Model' series of 'bullpup' automatic rifles. Bayonets derived from 'No.7 Mk.1/L' originals when 'Rifle, No.9' (EM2) and

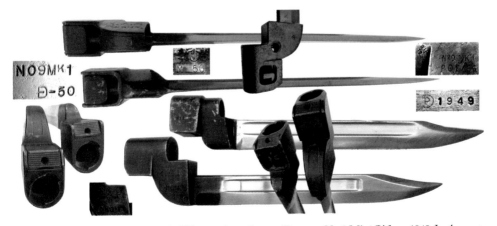

Fig. 166 Centre-left: Prototype bladed No.4 with, at the top, 'Bayonet, No.9 Mk.1/L' from 1949. In the centre of the image is a cut-away with mechanism. Inset markings: RSAF Enfield (E/D), ROF Poole (P), Pakistan Ordnance Factory (P.O.F.) and Byfords Ltd, West Bromwich (M.50). Issue markings for R.A.F Regiment, South Africa (U/arrow) and dates can also be seen.

'Bayonet, No.10 Mk.1' were adopted in April 1951. Political events forestalled the implementation when NATO-led calibre standardised agreement trials favoured the Belgian 7.62 mm round and Fabrique Nationale's *Fusil Automatique Légèr*. Based on Dieudonne J. Saive's experiments in England during the Second World War, the rifle (with knife bayonet) became Britain's 'Rifle, L1A1' on 1 February 1954.

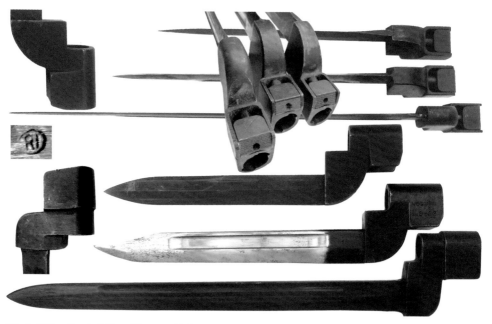

Fig. 167 Top: South African 'Bayonet, Rifle, 7,70mm (No.4 Mk.1)' from around the 1960s. Centre: 'Bayonet, No.9 Mk.1/L'. Bottom: Italian *Baionetta modificata compl. di fodero pe Enfield n.4*, from *c.* 1948. 'RI' stands for 'Repubblica Italiana'.

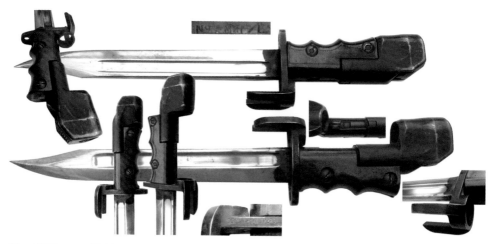

Fig. 168 'Bayonet, X1 E1' for 'Rifle 7 mm X1. E1' and '.30 inch X2. E1.', adopted in 1952 as 'Bayonet, No.10, Mk.1' with 'Rifle, EM2'. Cross-guard drawing number 'D.5(E).11490/A/276'. The catch is different to the 'No.7 Mk.1/L'.

Belgian FN FALs were utilised by over sixty countries by the 1980s. 'FAL Para' (50-61 to 50-64) and *Carabine Automatique Légère* (5.56-mm calibre – now *FNC*) utilised a 'Model C' tubular bayonet. This enclosed the long 22-mm flash hider/ grenade launcher. Two designs of catch developed. Argentina, Brazil, South Africa and Venezuela manufactured weapons under licence. South Africa and Israel adapted the design for the 'R4', 'Galil' and 'M16A1' rifles.

Switzerland's *Schweizerische Industrie Gesellschaft* developed an improved tubular bayonet for *Sturmgewehr (SG) 540* and *542* in around 1970. This featured heat-resistant plastic grips and guard with an aluminium pommel. France licensed a 1977 version from *Manurhin (Manufacture de Machines du Haut Rhin)*.

Britain still issued a socket bayonet with 'Rifle, L85A2' based on 'Enfield Weapons System' and 'Small Arms for the 80s' programmes. Experimental types for 'XL70' prototypes were displaced by Alec Newman's one-piece stainless steel investment casting. The side-muzzle, key-holed and toothed knife blade had an ergonomic socket with lever catch. Multi-tool functions involved a phenolite plastic scabbard with saw, sharpening stone and wire cutter assembly (blade pivot). The entire weapon received much battle experience in the Gulf War (1990/91), Iraq (2003) and Afghanistan (2001–14). The socket bayonet design now has unbroken service for over 300 years.

Fig. 169 Belgian-designed 'Model C' tubular bayonets for Fabrique Nationale's *Fusil* and *Carabine Automatique Léger*. At the bottom and to the right, it can be seen how the catch changed from a 'ridged' to a 'winged' version and the casting was simplified. Numerous nations used these. Inset: Dutch *Korps Mariniers* 'KM 3022', Argentinian *Ejército Argentino* '01-69932' and South African 'U/M17665' markings.

Fig. 170 Sleeved 'Model C' tubular bayonets for Israel's 'M16A1' to the left, and 'Galil', with rivet and in the centre of the image, rifles.

Fig. 171 Centre: South African 'R4' with new catch. Partial sleeves and reshaped blades tried. 'R1' markings 'U/M1137'.

Fig. 172 Swiss *Schweizerische Industrie Gesellschaft* tubular bayonet for *Sturmgewehr (SG) 540* and *542, c.* 1970. Olive-green heat-resistant plastic grips, guard and aluminium pommel. French copies named Manurhin (*Manufacture de Machines du Haut Rhin*) were made after 1977.

Fig. 173 Experimental 'XL70' series – drawing '29713/B'.

Fig. 174 Evolution of British 'Bayonet, L3A1' for 'Rifle, L85A1' & 'A2' from 1983 onwards. Top: Bottle-opener-style 1983 ('83 007'). Centre: New casting with rounded 'key-hole' of 1985 ('85 1448'). Bottom: The current model, with strengthened catch and cast mark on socket. In the lower left, the trials catch can be seen.

Conclusion – The Future?

Some nations dispensed with issue bayonets, except for ceremonial purposes, others continued to develop them. Britain's experiences in extremely hot environments stimulated 'Reducing the Burden' and a 'Lightweight Bayonet Requirement Competition'. Not adopted, an internal titanium structured 'Nylon Bayonet' was submitted by Riflecraft Ltd, Harleston in 2011. (US Patent 2012/0079753) The design for the 22-mm flash-hider may well be the last socket bayonet, but who can see into the future?

Fig. 175 Riflecraft Ltd's 'Nylon Bayonet'. White prototype with steel core and catchless example of titanium. Heatproof nylon aids camouflage and penetration through body armour. A standard 22-mm flash hider supports the socket.

Some Scabbards

Fig. 176 Left to right: 95, 107, 107, 117, 129, 107, 148, 138, 150.

Fig. 177 Top: 69. Left to right: 146, 141, 106, 126, 115, 126, 111, 137, 129, 113, 147.

Fig. 178 Left to right: 142, 125, 110, 109, 146, 144, 141, 122, 120, 119, 109, 96.

Fig. 179 Left: 168. Top to bottom: 157, 159, 159, 160, 164, 165, 174, 175, 173, 170, 170, 170.

Bibliography

Aarum, F., & Sægrov, S. G., *Døllebayonett I Norsk Bruk*, (Norway, Forsvarsmuseet, 1983).

Adam, G., Méry, C., Renoux, P., *Les baïonnettes militaires françaises*, (France, Crépin-Leblond, 2005).

Archives Nationale, Paris, Marine, portfeuille 223, pièce 65.

Blackmore, H. L., *British Military Firearms 1650–1850*, (London, Herbert Jenkins Ltd, 1961).

Bland, H., *Treatise of Military Discipline*, (London, 1727).

Calvó, J. L., *Armamento Reglamentario Y Auxilliar del Ejercito Español*, Libro No. 1, 'Modelos Portatiles de Avancarga 1717/1843', (Barcelona, 1975).

Chastenet, J. de, Chevalier, Seigneur de Puységur, *Memoires Historiques et Militaires sous Louis XIII et la Minorité de Louis XIV, Vol. 1*, (Paris, Chez Jacques Morel, 1690).

Dart, J., *Westmonasterium or the History of the Abbey Church of St Peter's Westminster*, (London, 1742).

Diderot, D. & d'Alembert J. le R., *Encyclopédie, ou dictionnaire raisonné des sciences, des arts et des métiers*, (Paris, 1751).

Durdik, J., Mudra, M., & Sada, M., *Firearms*, (London, Hamlyn Pub. Group, 1981).

Evans, R. D. C., *The Plug Bayonet: An Identification Guide for Collectors*, (Baildon, England, Private Pub., 2002).

Ezell, E. C., *The AK47 Story*, (USA, Stackpole Books, 1986).

Goldstein, E., *The Bayonet in New France 1665–1760*, (Canada, Museum Restoration Service, 1997).

Goldstein, E., *The Socket Bayonet in the British Army 1687–1783*, (Lincoln, USA, Andrew Mowbray Inc., 2000).

Gordon, A., *A Treatise on the Defence for the Sword, Bayonet and Pike in Close Action*, (London, 1805).

Götz, H. D., *Militärgewehre und Pistolen der deutschen Staaten 1800–1870*, (Stuttgart, Germany, Motorbuch Verlag, 1978).

Grant, J., *British Battles on Land and Sea, Vol. 2*, (London, Cassell & Co., 1897).

Grose, F., *Military Antiquities, Vol. 1*, (London, 1800).

Harding, D. F., *Smallarms of the East India Company 1600–1856* (4 vols), (London, Foresight Books, 1997, 1999).

Haswell, J., *The British Army*, (London, Thames & Hudson Ltd, 1975).

Huntington, R. T., *Hall's Breechloaders*, (York, USA, George Shumway, 1972).

Kulinsky, A. N., *Russian Edged Weapons, Polearms & Bayonets 18th-20th c.*, (St. Petersburg, Russia, 2001).

Lazard, P. E., *Vauban, 1633–1707*, (Paris, Librairie Felix Alcan, 1934).

Lissmark, B., *Svenska Bajonetter 1696–1965*, (Svenska Vapenstifelsen, Karlskrona, Sweden, 1979).

Løvschall, F., *Den Nye Th. Møller*, (Denmark, Devantier, 1997).

Mercaldo, L., *Allied Rifle Contracts in America*, (Greensboro, USA, Wet Dog Pub., 2011).

Wardman, W., *The Owen Gun*, (Australia, Curtin, 1991).

Pam, D., *The Royal Small Arms Factory Enfield & Its Workers*, (Enfield, 1998).

Priest, G., *The Bayonets of the Grand Master's Palace, Malta*, (England, Uppem Pub., 2003).

Priest, G., *The Brown Bess Bayonet 1720-1860*, (Norwich, Tharston Press, 1986).

Priest, G., *The Spirit of the Pike. British Socket Bayonets of the Twentieth Century*, (England, Uppem Pub., 2003).

Raw, S., *The Last Enfield*, (Cobourg, Canada, Collector Grade Publications Inc., 2003).

Reid, S., *British Redcoat 1740–1793*, (Oxford, Osprey Pub., 1996).

Reilly, R. M., *American Socket Bayonets and Scabbards*, (Rhode Island, USA, Andrew Mowbray Inc., 1990).

Saint Remy, P. Surirey de, *Memoires d' Artillerie, Vol. 1*, (Paris, Rollin, 1697).

Schmidt, P. A., *U.S Military Flintlock Muskets. The Later 1816 Through The Civil War*, (Woonsocket, USA, Andrew Mowbray Inc., 2007).

Schneider, H., & Meier J. A., *Griffwaffen*, (Zürich, Switzerland, Verlag-Stocker-Schmid, 1971).

Skennerton, I. D. & Richardson, R., *British and Commonwealth Bayonets*, (Margate, Australia, 1986).

Smid, J. & Moudry, P., *Bodáky Habsburské Monarchie 1683-1918*, (Prague, Czechoslovakia, Ars-Arm, 1994).

Stevens, R. B., & Van Rutten, J. E., *The Metric FAL*, (Toronto, Canada, Collector Grade Publications Inc., 1989).

Thierbach, M., *Die Geschichtliche Entwickelung der Handfeuerwaffe*, (Austria, Academische Druck, 1886).

Walter, J., *The German Bayonet*, (London, Arms & Armour Press, 1976).

Wardman, W., *The Owen Gun*, (Australia, Curtin, 1991)

Journals

Classic Arms & Militaria, Priest, G., 'An Exploration of the Firearm used by Killigrew's Dragoons in 1706', Vol. 8, No. 5, Sept./Oct. 2001, pp.26–30.

Gazette des Armes, Legen, J-L., 'La bataille de Denain ... il y a 300 ans', No. 446, October 2012, pp. 34–39.

Gazette des Armes, Legen, J-L., 'Les baïonnettes de la bataille de Denain (1712)', No. 456, Sept. 2013, pp. 36–41.

Journal of the United Services Institution, Scott, Capt. Sir S. D., 'On the history of the bayonet', Vol. 7, 1863.

Man at Arms for the Gun and Sword Collector, Priest, G., An Early "Bayonet Piece", Vol. 31 No. 2, March–April 2009, pp.30–38.

Man at Arms, Priest, G., '"Enfield" Bayonets in the Civil War 1861-65', Vol. 24 No. 2, April 2002, pp. 19–23, 42–47.

Man at Arms, Priest, G., 'Civil War Firearm & Bayonet Combinations of the Union & Confederacy: Austro-Hungarian Imports Examined', Vol. 25 No. 5, Sept. 2003, pp. 34–36.

Man at Arms, Priest, G., 'Civil War Longarm & Bayonet Combinations: The Less Famous European Imports (1861–1865)', Vol. 27 No. 6, Dec. 2005, pp. 24–27, 30–35, 38–41.

Man at Arms, Priest, G., 'The US Rifle-Musket Model of 1855 Bayonet in the Civil War', Vol. 33 No. 3, May 2011, pp. 23–26, 31–34, 39–42.

Man at Arms, Priest, G., 'Civil War Longarm & Bayonet Combinations: The Less Famous European Imports (1861–1865)', Vol. 27 No. 6, Dec. 2005, pp. 24–27, 30–35, 38 41.